Prospects for the UK Balance of Payments

Prospects for the UK Balance of Payments

Ken Coutts

and

Robert Rowthorn

Commentary

by

Bill Martin

Civitas: Institute for the Study of Civil Society
London

Published March 2010

Civitas
55 Tufton Street
London SW1P 3QL

Civitas is a registered charity (no. 1085494)
and a company limited by guarantee, registered in
England and Wales (no. 04023541)

email: books@civitas.org.uk

Independence: Civitas: Institute for the Study of Civil Society is a registered educational charity (No. 1085494) and a company limited by guarantee (No. 04023541). Civitas is financed from a variety of private sources to avoid over-reliance on any single or small group of donors.

All publications are independently refereed. All the Institute's publications seek to further its objective of promoting the advancement of learning. The views expressed are those of the authors, not of the Institute.

Typeset by
Civitas

Printed in Great Britain by
Cromwell Press Group
Trowbridge, Wiltshire

Contents

	Page
Authors	vi
Acknowledgements	vii
Abstract	viii
Prospects for the UK Balance of Payments	1
Figure 1: Balance of Payments Current Account (% GDP) old base projection: 1997-2007	2
Table 1: Main Items in the UK Current Account Balance of Payments 2008	5
Table 2: The Base Projection 2009-2020 Main Assumptions	6
Figure 2: UK Unemployment Rate (% of Labour Force) base projection	8
Figure 3: Balance of Payments Current Account (% GDP) base projection	9
Figure 4: Components of the Current Account (% GDP) base projection	9
Figure 5: Balance of Trade in Energy, Food & Basic Materials (% GDP) base projection	10
Figure 6: Net Investment Income (% GDP) base projection	10
Figure 7: Balance of Trade in Selected Services (% GDP) base projection	11
Table 3: Individual changes that improve the current account by 1% of GDP by 2020	12
Appendix: Sources and Methods	17
Commentary *Bill Martin*	21
References	27
Notes	29

Authors

Ken Coutts is Assistant Director of Research in the Faculty of Economics, University of Cambridge and Fellow in Economics, Selwyn College, Cambridge. His main research interests cover macroeconomic policy including fiscal and monetary policy, international trade and capital flows and balance of payments issues. He has published a number of articles on developments in Britain's balance of payments. He also does research on the behaviour of manufacturing prices and has published articles on the role of domestic and international competition on price setting by manufacturing firms.

Bill Martin is senior research associate at the Centre for Business Research, University of Cambridge. He was a special adviser in the Central Policy Review Staff between 1981 and 1983 and a Special Adviser to the House of Commons Treasury Select Committee between 1986 and 1997. Until 2004, he was Chief Economist at the fund management arm of UBS. He continues to research in the field of macroeconomics and is a member of the Financial Services Consumer Panel.

Robert Rowthorn is Emeritus Professor of Economics and Fellow of King's College, Cambridge. He is the author a number of academic articles on economic growth, structural change and the balance of payments. His books include, *De-industrialisation and Foreign Trade* (with John Wells). He has been a consultant on these topics for a variety of bodies including the International Monetary Fund, the UN Commission on Trade and Development, the International Labour Organisation and the British government.

Acknowledgements

This paper is based on research carried out at the Centre for Business Research, Cambridge, as part of the *Services Innovation* project at the UK Innovation Research Centre (UK~IRC) at Cambridge and Imperial College. The UK~IRC is co-funded by the Department for Business, Innovation and Skills (BIS), the Economic and Social Research Council (ESRC), the National Endowment for Science, Technology and the Arts (NESTA) and the Technology Strategy Board (TSB). The support of all these organisations is gratefully acknowledged.

We should like to thank Wynne Godley, Alan Hughes and Bill Martin for their helpful comments.

Abstract

This paper presents disaggregated projections for the UK balance of payments up to 2020. Under conservative assumptions about underlying trends it is projected that the current account deficit will increase from 2% of GDP in 2009 to almost 5% of GDP by the end of the period. Empirical evidence indicates that a deficit of this magnitude is not sustainable and, if unchecked, will lead to a painful adjustment involving lost output and higher unemployment. The paper calls for industrial and other policies to improve UK trade performance, above all in manufacturing, but also in knowledge-intensive services (communications, consultancy, R&D, media etc). It also points out the need to safeguard London's role as a global financial centre.

Journal of Economic Literature **(JEL) Codes:** F14; F17; F37; L60; L80

Keywords: Balance of Payments, forecasts; visible trade; services; investment income; industrial policy.

Prospects for the UK Balance of Payments

Over the past sixty years the UK economy has undergone huge structural changes.[1] In 1950 this country was a great industrial power with more than a third of its labour force employed in the manufacturing sector and a further million in coal mining. There was a trade surplus in manufactured goods equal to 10% of GDP and the country was a net exporter of energy. Since then, employment in the manufacturing sector has shrunk dramatically and coal mining has almost disappeared. There is now a trade deficit in manufactured goods equal to 4% of GDP and, after an interlude following the discovery of North Sea oil, the UK is now a large net importer of energy. The gap left by the decline of our traditional industries has been filled by a whole range of service activities, which now account for the bulk of employment and, collectively, earn a valuable trade surplus. In addition, the country enjoys significant net earnings in the form of interest, profits and dividends from international investment.

The costs and benefits of these changes, and what could or should have been done about them, were at one time hotly debated. However, such concerns were eventually buried under the euphoria of a prolonged economic boom and a bubble in house and share prices. They have now resurfaced following the credit crisis and ensuing recession. There is a widespread feeling that something has gone wrong, that the economy has become dangerously unbalanced, and we have put too much faith in finance at the expense of manufacturing and other activities. There are also new concerns about food and energy security in the face of rising world demand and limited supplies.

Previous Projections

Some years ago a small group of us in Cambridge, under the aegis of the Centre for Business Research, set out to investigate the role of manufacturing in the UK economy.[2] The manufacturing sector had been shedding jobs for some decades and the pace of decline had been faster than in other countries. The official index of production indicated that the aggregate output of UK manufacturing had been stagnating for nearly twenty years, whereas many other countries had experienced considerable growth in production. Was this situation sustainable over the longer term? In particular, was it compatible with the sound balance of payments required for national solvency? Would manufacturing exports be sufficient in the future to pay for the imports we require? If not, what alternative sources of income would be available to bridge the gap?

Figure 1: Balance of Payments Current Account (% GDP) old base projection: 1997-2007

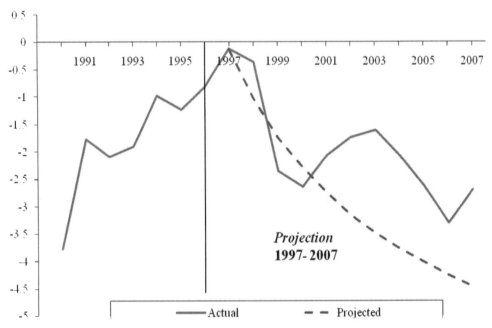

We began our investigations at a time when the UK balance of payments had been improving for some years. The current account balance as a whole was close to zero (Figure 1). There was a small deficit on manufacturing trade and a small surplus on the totality of other current items. Our objective was to investigate whether this satisfactory state of affairs would continue, and to see if there were underlying trends that might disrupt this equilibrium and give rise to serious payments difficulties in the future. Our starting point was the "base projection".[3] This projection represented our best estimate of what would happen over a ten year horizon in the absence of policy changes or shocks. This is a much longer horizon than is usually attempted in macroeconomic forecasting. Under the base projection there was a steady deterioration in the overall current account culminating in a deficit equal to 4.5% of GDP in 2007. In the event, the current account did deteriorate but by less than projected.

2

In evaluating our projection, it is useful to consider manufactures and non-manufactured items separately. We projected that the trade balance in manufactures would get steadily worse, culminating in a deficit of around 4% of GDP in 2007. This turned out to be an accurate forecast, and our projection of the manufacturing balance tracked closely what actually happened.[4] We also projected a worsening situation on the non-manufacturing side of the account. This turned out to be wrong, which explains why the current account as a whole performed somewhat better than expected.

In recent years, the behaviour of the non-manufacturing side of the current account has been dominated by the following items, all of which have been subject to large changes that we did not foresee:

- *Finance ("The City")*. Net overseas earnings of the financial sector have been on an upward trend for a considerable time. Starting in 2005 there was also a spectacular boom in which these earnings rose by 60% within the space of two years. Our projections got the upward trend, but not the recent boom.

- *Investment income*. Net investment income has fluctuated widely over the years. During our projection period, net income was boosted by a wave of cross-border mergers and acquisitions through which UK firms trebled their highly profitable stock of overseas assets. Towards the end of the period, net income was also inflated by the huge and unexpected losses sustained by certain foreign banks operating in London.[5] Our projections underestimated the growth of net income because we failed to anticipate either of these developments.

- *Energy, food and basic materials*. For some time before and after our projections began in 1997, the UK had a modest deficit on trade in these items. Net earnings from trade in energy (oil, gas, coal and electricity) were outweighed by expenditure on imported food, minerals and the like, but the gap was quite small as a percentage of GDP. However, from the turn of the century onwards the situation become much worse under the impact of falling North Sea oil production and rising import prices. Our projections took into account the fall in oil production but not the large price increases.

3

The above errors illustrate some of the pitfalls involved in long-term forecasting and highlight the inherent uncertainty surrounding major items in the balance of payments.[6] Without the unforeseen growth in overseas investment income and the recent boom in City earnings, there would have been a much larger deficit in the current account at the end of the projection period in 2007. Conversely, without the unexpected rise in import prices for energy, food and materials, the current account would have been close to balance in 2007. With hindsight, these developments can be explained, but they were not widely foreseen at the time.

Looking to the Future

The fate of our original projections is now water under the bridge. What about the future? What are the prospects for the UK balance of payments? To what extent will national solvency in the future depend on the strength of the manufacturing sector? What is likely to be the performance of this sector in the absence of major new policy initiatives? If manufacturing performs badly, will other sectors be able to fill the gap and generate the income required to pay for our imports? These are the questions the CBR group in Cambridge explored in our original projections. After more than a decade, we are now revisiting this topic and in the current paper we present a new set of projections for the period 2009-2020.[7] These projections come with a health warning. As we have seen above, some of the main items in the balance of payments are subject to great uncertainty and any longer term projection, such as ours, is therefore subject to a large margin of error.

A projection is a conditional forecast. It does not say what will actually happen. It forecasts what *would* happen under certain assumptions about government policy and the behaviour of a number of economic variables, such as the price of oil or the growth of world trade. Different assumptions yield different forecasts.[8] We start from the "base projection", which assumes no change in government policy and embodies a set of assumptions about broad economic trends that seem reasonable in the light of existing evidence. We then examine how varying some of the main assumptions would affect the projected outcomes. Such an exercise helps to identify potential sources of error and quantifies their relative importance. It also indicates the potential importance of various policy interventions to strengthen the balance of payments.

A full description of the projections is given in an appendix and here we describe only their main features.

4

Table 1 lists the main items in the current account. The headings shown are similar to those in our earlier projections. Most of them are self-explanatory. The main difference is that a separate category of "knowledge-intensive" services is identified. This heading covers a huge variety of services such as communications, construction, computer & information services, royalties and license fees, consultancy, R&D, audio-visual services etc. It excludes financial services and insurance. Knowledge-intensive services were previously lumped together with transport, travel and government services, but this is no longer appropriate given their increasing importance in the balance of payments.

Table 1: Main Items in the UK Current Account Balance of Payments 2008 (£ millions)

	Credits	Debits	Balance	%GDP
Surplus Items				
Financial services & insurance	60,864	15,282	45,582	3.2
Other knowledge-intensive services	66,955	38,944	28,011	1.9
Investment income	262,671	235,025	27,646	1.9
Deficit Items				
Manufactures	193,601	251,449	-57,848	-4.0
Energy (oil, coal, electricity & gas etc)	35,386	47,841	-12,455	-0.9
Food, beverages and tobacco	13,719	31,099	-17,380	-1.2
Basic materials	6,625	11,014	-4,389	-0.3
Transport and travel	40,478	57,632	-17,154	-1.2
Government services	2,102	4,062	-1,960	-0.1
Current transfers	15,422	29,032	-13,610	-0.9
Items not elsewhere specified	2,803	4,314	-1,511	-0.1
Current Account	**700,626**	**725,694**	**-25,068**	**-1.7**

Source: *UK Balance of Payments Pink Book 2009*, ONS; table 1.2, 2.1, 3.1.

Table 2: The Base Projection 2009-2020 Main Assumptions

Real domestic spending grows at 1.5% p.a. in 2010, 2.5% p.a. in 2011 and 3% p.a. thereafter.

World trade grows at 3% p.a. in 2011 and 5% p.a. thereafter.

Real price of oil increases at 2% p.a. in 2010 and 2.5 % p.a. thereafter.

Real price of food increases at 2% p.a. from 2010.

Volume of oil production falls by 7% p.a. from 2010.

Real balance on basic materials and other energy worsens by 0.05% of GDP annually.

Balance of financial services falls by 0.5% of GDP in 2009 from its peak in 2008.

Real exchange rate constant at the 2008 level throughout.

Base Projection: Assumptions

The main assumptions underlying the base projection are shown in Table 2. Further details are given in an appendix. In addition we assume that there is no change in government policy. The following are some points to note:

- *Exchange Rate.* The exchange rate plays an important role in the projections for trade in manufactures and also for certain other items such as trade in food and the valuation of overseas assets. We assume that the devaluation that took place in 2007-2008 is maintained throughout the projection period.

- *World Trade.* UK manufacturing exports are closely linked to world trade. We assume that world trade grows at 5% p.a. from 2010 onwards. This is similar to the historic trend.

- *Financial services.* Trade statistics for the first half of 2009 suggest there has been some fall in net earnings from financial services (ONS 2009, table F).[9] Taking a longer view, it is likely that global finance will become more regulated, more conservative, and on average less profitable than in the past. In themselves, such changes may harm the City and damage UK financial exports. However, they should be seen against the wider background of world economic growth. The current

6

recession is coming to an end and prospects for UK financial exports should improve as the world economy recovers. Whatever happens in the short term, the longer term prospect is for continued growth in net earnings from financial services, perhaps at a slower pace than before. This is what our projection assumes.

- *Investment income.* This is a highly volatile item and it is difficult to know what will happen to it in the future. UK net income from investment was inflated in 2007-2008 by the huge losses of foreign banks operating in London. In line with the Treasury, we assume that net investment income falls back sharply in 2009.[10] Thereafter we assume, in line with past experience, that the rate of return on UK overseas assets is somewhat higher than on UK liabilities.[11]

- *Energy, food and basic materials.* These are also difficult items to predict. Our projection assumes that North Sea oil production falls at 7% p.a. after 2010. This is midway between the government's base case (9.0% p.a. after 2012) and the slower decline case (5.0% p.a. after 2009).[12] What will happen to prices in the short-run is highly uncertain. Over the long-run it is likely that world population growth plus rising incomes and falling reserves will lead a large and permanent increase in the world prices of energy, food and materials.[13] We assume that the *real* prices of oil and food will increase by 2.5% p.a. and 2% p.a. respectively from 2010 onwards. We also assume that the balance of trade in basic materials and other energy deteriorates at a trend rate equal to 0.05% of GDP per annum over the period as a whole.

Base Projection: Results

The main results for the base projection are as follows:

- *Unemployment* (ILO definition): after rising to a peak of just over 10% unemployment falls back again to 6.3% in 2020. This compares to a pre-crisis figure of around 5% (Figure 2).

7

Figure 2: UK Unemployment Rate (% of Labour Force) base projection

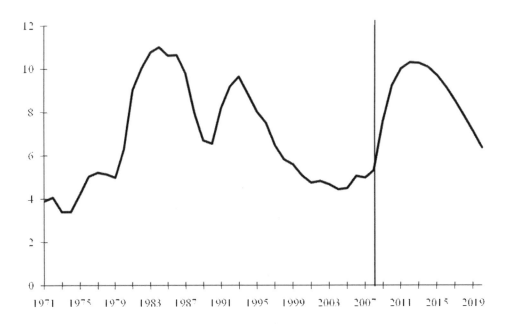

- *Balance of Payments Current Account:* this deteriorates fairly steadily to reach a deficit equal to 4.7% of GDP by 2020 (Figure 3).

- *Manufactures:* the deficit on manufacturing trade initially improves because of devaluation, but this improvement is not sustained and the deficit eventually gets larger (Figure 4).

- *Other items*: the non-manufacturing side of the balance of payments is initially in surplus, but this is eventually transformed into a small deficit (Figure 4). This turnaround is due to the growing deficits in oil, food, basic materials and other energy, under the influence of adverse price and production trends (Figure 5). The most important factor is the increase in oil imports due to the rapid decline of North Sea production.

- *Investment income:* Net income from investment falls sharply in 2009 and from then onwards remains roughly constant as a fraction of GDP throughout the projection period (Figure 6).

8

Figure 3: Balance of Payments Current Account (% GDP) base projection

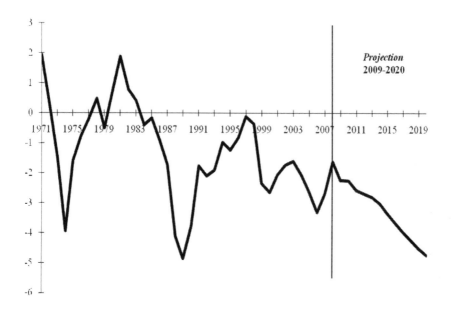

Figure 4: Components of the Current Account (% GDP) base projection

Figure 5: Balance of Trade in Energy, Food & Basic Materials (% GDP) base projection

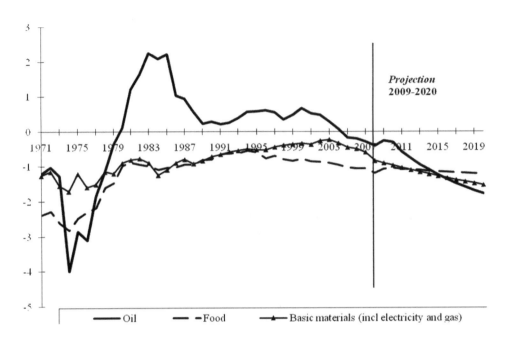

Figure 6: Net Investment Income (% GDP) base projection

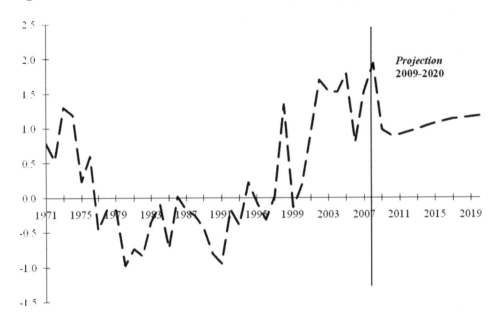

- *Services*: Taken as a whole, services enjoy a large and growing surplus. Within this total, "traditional" services (transport, travel and government) are in persistent deficit (Figure 7). Net earnings from finance initially decline due to the credit crunch, but then gradually recover. There is also a sustained increase in net earnings from other knowledge-intensive services.

Figure 7: Balance of Trade in Selected Services (% GDP) base projection

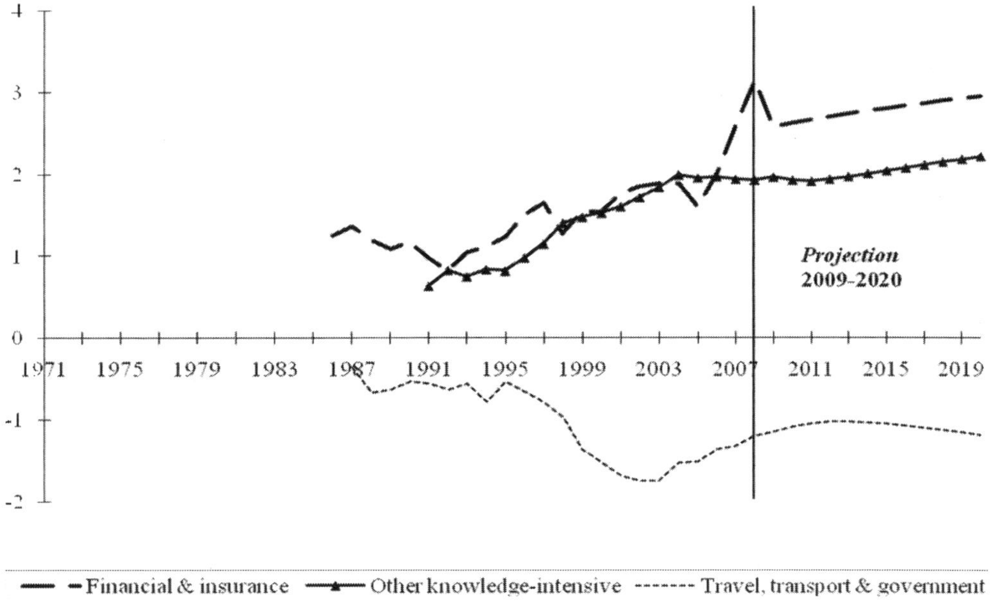

Base Projection: Sensitivity Analysis

The above is a rather gloomy picture. After a decade of economic recovery and growth, the unemployment rate is approaching its pre-crisis level. However, there is a large current account deficit equal to almost 5% of GDP. A deficit of this magnitude has been observed only once before in the modern era, for a brief period in 1989. The base projection will almost certainly be wrong, but the interesting questions are how wrong and for what reason?

11

Table 3: Individual changes that improve the current account by 1% of GDP by 2020

	BASE PROJECTION	NEW ASSUMPTION
Real competitiveness (relative unit labour costs) change	0	-12.5%
Real oil price increase	+2.5% p.a.	-3.5% p.a.
Volume of oil production change	-7% p.a.	-2.7% p.a.
Growth of domestic spending (implied unemployment rate 2.3 percentage points above base projection in 2020)	3% p.a.	2.35% p.a.
Growth of world trade	5% p.a.	6.5% p.a.
Long-term real return on UK overseas assets	1.9% p.a.	2.3% p.a.
Average growth of real net exports of financial and insurance services (28% above base projection by 2020)*	0.1% p.a.	2.4% p.a.
Average growth of real net exports of other knowledge-intensive (35% above base projection by 2020)*	1.8% p.a.	4.1% p.a.
Average growth of manufactured exports (9.5% above base projection by 2020)**	4.8% p.a.	5.7% p.a.

NOTE: CALCULATED BY MODIFYING THE RELEVANT ASSUMPTION IN THE BASE PROJECTION. EACH MODIFICATION LEADS TO A 1% OF GDP IMPROVEMENT IN THE BALANCE OF PAYMENTS ON CURRENT ACCOUNT BY 2020. *REAL QUANTITIES ARE DERIVED BY DEFLATING NOMINAL QUANTITIES BY THE GDP DEFLATOR. **VOLUME INDEX DERIVED BY DEFLATING NOMINAL EXPORTS BY THE PRICE DEFLATOR FOR MANUFACTURED EXPORTS; TAKES INTO ACCOUNT THE FACT THAT AN INCREASE IN MANUFACTURED EXPORTS INDUCES MORE IMPORTS.

When projecting the future balance of payments what matters is not just the growth rate of any particular item, but also its initial size. The two largest items by a long way are manufactured goods and income from overseas investment (Table 1). Despite all the changes that have occurred, manufactured exports are still three times as large as the total export earnings of the entire City of London or of the whole gamut of other knowledge-intensive services. An instant ten% rise in manufactured exports combined with a similar fall in manufactured imports would generate a £45 billion improvement in the balance of payments, which is more than UK net earnings from financial services and insurance. An instant ten% reduction in the amount of investment income we receive combined with a ten% increase in what we pay out, would lead to a net loss of £50 billion.

These are huge figures. They are similar in magnitude to what our imports of fuels would cost if North Sea oil dried up overnight and energy prices returned to their peak value of 2008.

Table 3 provides further information on this issue. It shows how sensitive our overall balance of payments projection is to unforeseen shocks or variations in the assumptions which underlie the base projection. It lists a number of changes that would individually cause an improvement in the current account balance in 2020 equal to 1% of GDP. These are as follows:

- *Domestic Demand.* The base projection assumes that domestic spending grows at 3.0% p.a. If spending were to grow at 2.35% p.a. instead, this would eventually reduce the balance of payments deficit by 1% of GDP. Because of the slower growth in demand the unemployment rate in 2020 would be 2.3 percentage points (800,000) higher than under the base projection. In human terms expenditure restraint is a costly way of preserving national solvency.

- *Devaluation.* The base projection assumes that the real exchange rate remains constant throughout the projection period. A permanent devaluation of 12.5% would eventually improve the balance of payments by 1% of GDP. This devaluation would be on top of the large currency devaluations that have already occurred during 2007-08.

- *World Trade.* The base projection assumes that world trade grows by 5% p.a. If it were to grow instead by 6.5% p.a., this would produce the required improvement in the balance of payments.

- *Real Oil Price.* The base projection assumes that the real oil price increases by 2.5% a year. To produce the required improvement in the balance of payments would require the real oil price to *fall* by an average of 3.5% p.a. over the entire projection period. This is conceivable, but unlikely.

- *UK Oil Production.* The base projection assumes, optimistically, that UK oil production will fall by 7% p.a. To generate the required improvement in the balance of payments would require oil production to fall by only 2.7% a year. In 2020 the UK would still be producing almost three quarters as much oil as in 2008. This is a remote possibility.

- *Return on overseas assets.* An increase of 0.4 percentage points on UK investments abroad would generate an additional net income in 2020 equal to 1% of GDP. This calculation assumes there is no change in the return that foreigners obtain on their investments in the UK. Such a positive shock cannot be ruled out, although neither can a shock in the opposite direction. The future behaviour of net investment income is highly uncertain.

- *Financial and Insurance Services.* An additional 28% in net export earnings from this sector by 2020 would be equivalent to 1% of GDP. This would be an impressive achievement.

- *Other knowledge-intensive services.* An additional 35% in net earnings from other knowledge-intensive services by 2020 would be equivalent to 1% of GDP. To achieve this result would require such earnings to grow more than twice as fast as we envisage under the base projection. This is unlikely.

- *Manufactured exports.* An additional 9.5% in manufactured exports would improve the current account by 1% of GDP in 2020. This calculation takes into account the fact that manufactured exports have a high import content.

If all or most of the above changes to the base projection were to occur simultaneously, then by 2020 the UK would enjoy a current account surplus. Conversely, if similar changes were to occur simultaneously in the opposite direction, there would be a gigantic current account deficit. The above calculations illustrate the sensitivity of our projections to two particular items: investment income and manufacturing trade. As Table 1 indicates, these are very large items and relatively small proportionate errors in projecting their behaviour will have a substantial impact on the balance of payments. This is not the case for most of the other items in the balance of payments, which are mostly much smaller in magnitude.

Discussion

The base projection represents our best estimate of what will happen over the next decade if present trends continue. It paints a rather gloomy picture. By

2020, the unemployment rate is almost back to its pre-crisis level. However, the projected current account deficit is almost 5% of GDP. Excluding investment income, the deficit is almost 6%. Do deficits of this magnitude matter? Most economists agree that countries cannot run large current account deficits forever, because of the resulting growth of foreign debt; sooner or later some form of adjustment will be required. The question is how large is large and how painful will the eventual adjustment be? C. Fred Bergsten (2002) has argued that "research at both the Federal Reserve Board and the Institute for International Economics reveals that industrial countries, including the United States, enter a danger zone of current account unsustainability when their deficits reach 4 - 5 percent of GDP... At these levels, corrective forces tend to arise either spontaneously from market forces or by policy action." More recent research by Clarida *et al* (2007) reaches the same conclusion. In their econometric analysis of industrial countries, Freund and Warnock (2007) find that deficit adjustment typically involves a decrease in GDP growth and may involve currency depreciation. They also find that larger deficits take longer to adjust and are associated with significantly slower output growth (relative to trend) during the current account recovery than smaller deficits. These various findings suggest that deficits on the scale we project are a cause for concern. If our projection turns out to be correct there may eventually be a painful adjustment involving loss of output and rising unemployment.

As we have stressed throughout this paper, there is a great deal of uncertainty in forecasting over such a long time period. However, there are grounds for believing that underlying trends are moving against the UK. Imports of energy are almost certain to rise considerably as UK oil production falls, and the cost of imported energy, food and basic materials are also likely to increase. This would not matter if there were offsetting improvements elsewhere in the balance of payments. As things stand at the moment, it is difficult to see where the required improvements would come from. The base projection takes a rather optimistic view of the service sector, yet as a proportion of GDP the overall trade balance in services is only a little greater in 2020 than it was at the start of the period in 2008. Net income from investment falls under this projection and, after an initial improvement, the trade deficit in manufactures gets larger.

The relentless deterioration in the balance of payments that occurs under the base projection is not sustainable. Some of the trends are beyond our control, but there are at least three important areas where government policy could make a difference. These are: the City of London, manufacturing and other knowledge-intensive services. As far as the City is concerned, future reform of the financial sector should be designed so as to contribute to the export potential of this sector. In the case of manufacturing and knowledge-intensive services, there is scope for what might be loosely called an "industrial policy". This is now coming back into fashion, although what it would mean in practice is at present rather vague and subject to debate. There is also the exchange rate to consider. The big devaluation that occurred in 2007-08 has given UK exporters an advantage and the government should aim to preserve this advantage by pursuing appropriate monetary and fiscal policies. Indeed, to the extent that it is feasible, there is a case for engineering a further sterling devaluation.

Given the orders of magnitude involved, any policy for dealing with the emerging balance of payments deficit must assign a central role to manufacturing. The scale of UK trade in manufactures is, and will remain for years to come, several times larger than the exports of the City of London and all knowledge-intensive services put together. Safeguarding the City and increasing knowledge-intensive exports are both important objectives, but success in these areas would not remove the need to improve the trade performance of the manufacturing sector.

The opposition between manufacturing and services is to some extent a false one. In a modern economy like ours, the dividing line between manufacturing and services is becoming increasingly blurred. Many manufacturing firms rely heavily on knowledge-intensive services provided by outside suppliers, whereas some manufacturing firms are also major service providers in their own right. It would be difficult to conceive of a viable industrial policy for manufacturing that did not also involve knowledge-intensive services. With a stronger manufacturing sector, there would be a larger internal market for manufacturing-related services, and access to this market would enable UK service providers to benefit from economies of scale and develop skills which can be exploited in export markets.

There is a precautionary motive for policies to strengthen the balance of payments. Our projections are surrounded by a great deal of uncertainty and, although things could turn out better than we project, there is a fair chance they could turn out significantly worse. Simply on grounds of prudence there is a case for industrial and other policies designed boost UK trade performance.

Appendix: Sources and Methods

Our model is a convenient information system for making alternative conditional projections of the balance of payments, its main components and some macroeconomic aggregates of the UK Economy.

Table A1: The Balance of Payments and its main components

		CURRENT ACCOUNT (FLOWS)
1.	Visible Trade	
		Food, beverages and tobacco
		Oil
		Basic materials and other energy
		Manufactures
2.	Invisible Trade	
		Traditional services[1]
		Knowledge-intensive services[2]
		Financial services[3]
3.	Income	
		Investment income (credits and debits)
		Net current transfers and remittances
		Capital and Financial Account
		Transactions in real and financial assets and liabilities[4]
		Net capital transfers
		International Investment Position (Stocks)
		Balance sheets: assets and liabilities

[1] Transportation, travel and government services

[2] Communications, construction, computer and information technology, royalties and licence fees, other business, personal cultural and recreational, communications.

[3] Finance and insurance ("The City").

[4] Direct investment, portfolio investment and other financial securities.

17

Visible trade is divided into four categories. Trade in oil includes crude oil and petroleum products, but other energy products are allocated to basic materials. Trade in services has been divided into three groups. The Traditional Services balance, which includes sea and air transport and travel (tourism), has long been in deficit. Knowledge-intensive services cover a wide range of activities and have made a growing contribution to net service exports. The balance of Financial Services (including insurance) is the other large surplus component of trade in services. Investment income is the aggregate of direct investment, portfolio investment and other securities, divided into the banking and non-banking sectors. The remaining category is net current transfers and compensation of employees (remittances). The balance of all these transactions is the balance of payments on current account.

Purchases and sales of assets and liabilities provide the link between the current account and the balance sheet. We distinguish between the banking and non-banking sectors in the flows of capital and in the (end-year) stocks of assets and liabilities of domestic residents with overseas residents. All the balance of payments data comes from the Office for National Statistics Pink Book (United Kingdom Balance of Payments: 2008 Edition), supplemented by trade statistics and quarterly balance of payments data. The balance of payments analysis is linked to major macroeconomics aggregates such as GDP and employment. National accounts aggregates come from United Kingdom National Accounts (Blue Book, 2008 Edition), supplemented by quarterly national accounts. Employment and other labour market data come from Labour Market Statistics, published by the Office for National Statistics (ONS). All the data is available from the ONS web site url: http://www.statistics.gov.uk/.

Model structure and properties
Table A2

ENDOGENOUS VARIABLES of which:				
		64		
	identities	49	inexact equations	15
EXOGENOUS		**26**		
Total		90		

Since there are 90 variables in the model and 64 independent equations relating to subsets of these variables, we can treat 26 variables as exogenous, i.e. not "explained" by the model. A projection is a solution of the 64 endogenous variables for each year of the projection period, conditional on assumptions about the exogenous variables (a time-path for each exogenous variable over the projection period).

Most of the structure of the model consists of accounting identities relating to the various components of the balance of payments. The inexact equations summarise behavioural relationships over the historic period from 1971-2008 and include a residual between the actual historical value of the endogenous variable and the value calculated from the equation. For the projection period we must make assumptions about the future value of the residual. A common assumption is to project the last observed residual in 2008 so that there is a smooth transition from the 2008 value of the variable to its forecast value for 2009 and beyond. Of the 15 inexact equations, there are 12 equations for which we can establish reasonably stable long-run relationships; they include trade volumes, trade prices, the domestic expenditure deflator and employment. For the remaining equations (which include net financial services) we have been unable to explain past behaviour satisfactorily in any systematic way. These variables are projected on the basis of historic trends and assumptions about the residuals.

Exogenous variables

The principal exogenous variables in the conditional forecasts divide into six groups. They are: the volume of domestic expenditure; the index of wages and salaries per unit of output; the nominal exchange rate and relative unit labour costs; the price and volume of oil; the world demand for manufactured goods; the real returns on external assets and liabilities. Our "base projection" assumptions are summarised in Table 2. The sensitivity analysis summarised in Table 3 is obtained by calculating alternative solutions of the model to vary the exogenous variables by the amounts required to achieve a 1% of GDP improvement in the current account. For this exercise, the current account is "the target" and the exogenous variable is "the instrument".

19

Principal Behavioural Relationships

Export and import volumes of manufactures depend upon income and relative cost elasticities. Export volumes are related to an index of the volume of world demand for manufactures, weighted by the UK share in each market. The series is derived from OECD *Economic Outlook*, 2009, Annex Table 53. Import volumes depend both upon the volume of domestic expenditure and the volume of exports, so that faster export growth draws in more imports of manufactures. Exports and imports both depend on an index of normalised relative unit labour costs expressed in common currency, published in IMF *Financial Statistics*. Changes in the real exchange rate (as measured by the IMF normalised relative unit labour cost index) gradually affect trade volumes, so that the full effect of devaluation on the volume of exports or imports takes about four years to complete. Trade prices depend upon the domestic price index and relative unit labour costs. Our measure of inflation is based on the domestic expenditure deflator, which depends on unit wage and salary costs and import prices. The equation has the long-run property that when unit wage costs and import prices are growing at the same rate, domestic inflation is also growing at this rate.

Investment income is projected on assumptions about real rates of return on assets and liabilities and on capital gains or losses on the stocks of assets and liabilities. The current account balance then determines changes in the net stock of external assets.

Employment depends on GDP and a trend to capture long-run productivity growth associated with technical progress. The long-run employment to output elasticity is close to unity, but employment adjusts with a lag to output changes, so that short-run productivity is strongly pro-cyclical. The workforce is exogenous and unemployment is derived from the projection for employment and the workforce.

Commentary

Bill Martin

I begin by declaring an interest. Last year I wrote that the UK had a latent balance of payments problem and argued that the authorities should pursue a cheap currency policy, supported if necessary by direct foreign currency intervention.[1] So I am afraid I am not an unbiased commentator on Ken and Bob's strategic analysis, with which I fundamentally agree.

The basic story they tell is not an unfamiliar one. They say that the UK is poorly placed given current trends and levels of competitiveness to fill the external hole left by the prospective run down in North Sea oil and gas production. What the authors bring to this story is rigour and a good sense of orders of magnitude.

Their calculations show not an imminent crisis but a slow and steady deterioration in the current account as a percent of GDP of 3 percentage points between 2008 and 2020. This is not a conventional forecast of the balance of payments at a particular date; the projection is better regarded as a depiction of a broad tendency. Of the 3-percentage point deterioration, no less than 2 percentage points comes from the balance in oil and basic materials, including gas. In other words, the rundown in the North Sea coupled with rising real oil prices accounts for most of the projected deterioration. Another ½ percentage point comes from a worse balance in manufactures.

The authors project the continuation of an upward trend in the overall trade surplus in services. This is not apparent from the comparison with 2008 but it is clear if the comparison is taken from 2007. In 2008, the banks' trade surplus was artificially inflated by the large gap between banks' deposit and lending rates, the result of the banking crisis. This artificial boost has since gradually disappeared.

The remaining part of the authors' projected current account deterioration comes from lower investment income, which they admit is nigh impossible to forecast. The UK's investment income was inflated in 2008 and 2009 by the collapse in redistributed profits of foreign banks operating in the UK. So neither year would be a good place from which to start one's projections. The authors' 2020 projection for investment income as a share of GDP is close to the average seen in 2006 and 2007. I think this must imply some increase in the private sector component of investment income since the government will be paying more interest on that part of its rising debt held by foreigners.

To add some balance to my otherwise biased commentary, I shall now pose a few sceptical questions. The first is why we should worry at all about the current account of the balance of payments. We are largely indifferent to the balance of payments of individual regions within the United Kingdom so why should we be concerned by the imbalance that arises between the UK and the Rest of the World?

Part of the answer is that the regions are protected from the impact of shifting international capital flows in a way that the UK is not. The state offers protection, explicit and implicit, to individual regions. The economy is less well protected. Capital inflows required to finance a deficit may stop, possibly abruptly, if there are mounting imagined currency or default risks. The capital stop might inflict a painful adjustment process, including a prolonged period of unemployment. This is the message of the international studies that the authors cite. The study by Clarida and others[2] suggests that the UK crosses into the danger zone when the current account deficit exceeds a figure below 2% of GDP – much less than the authors are projecting. The policy conclusion is that a succession of large current account deficits financed by unreliable capital flows is best avoided.

A second response to the sceptic's question is to acknowledge that not all large current account deficits are of concern. Whether the economy is vulnerable to capital stops depends entirely on the underlying causes of the balance of payment deficit. The deficit may have wholly benign underpinnings. An economy enjoying the fruits of innovation might well run a current account deficit, as domestic investment plans outstrip planned saving. External capital inflows can sustainably bridge the domestic planned investment saving gap. This is essentially the story that was told to excuse the emergence of America's rising current account deficit during the late 1990s.

The growing UK balance of payment deficit traced by the authors is not however the result of a presumed surge in Britain's rate of technical progress. Rather it is a symptom of an adjustment failure – the inability given current trends and levels of competitiveness of the non-oil economy to make good the impact of oil's retreat.

The key question therefore is whether the authors have got their sums right. They rightly emphasise the huge uncertainties and are disarmingly honest about their last attempt, which they describe warts and all. In this context, I would like to have seen a more formal test of the model they use. Their projections are a mixture of modelling and forecasters' judgement, and it would have been useful to know how well the model itself tracks the past and forecasts out of sample.

Although the authors perfectly understand this point, readers of their paper could be forgiven for not fully grasping the mechanism that prevents the non-oil economy from filling the balance of payments hole left by oil's decline. Readers will understand that further improvements in competitiveness as a result of devaluation are ruled out by assumption. But they might be puzzled why, for example, the manufacturing balance having improved in the first part of the projection period, thanks to devaluation, then begins steadily to deteriorate.

One reason is that the authors assume a slightly faster pace of growth in domestic spending in the second part of the projection period. But the more important reason is a presumed structural feature of the UK, its tendency to suck in more imports than it generates in exports. To put the point more formally, the model builds in a disparity in income trade elasticities: the growth in imports of manufactures induced by an increase in UK income is higher that the growth in exports of manufactures induced by a comparable increase in overseas income. In the model, the import elasticity for manufactures is roughly twice the size of the effective export elasticity.[3]

Is this a plausible feature on which to base projections of the UK's balance of payments? I would argue that it is. Houthakker and Magee[4] were probably the first econometricians to have uncovered forty years ago a similar disparity in the UK's trade elasticities. Despite best efforts, many, although not all, studies since have uncovered the same phenomenon. Its precise cause and interpretation is open to debate. But taken at face value, it implies that to secure a non-deteriorating trade account with unchanged levels of competitiveness the UK has to grow less quickly than its trading partners. Should it grow more quickly, there would be a tendency for the balance of payments to deteriorate. *I believe the boom in oil and the boom in finance may well have disguised this underlying structural problem.*

Sceptics will suspect that the authors are too pessimistic in their projections, especially on investment income where revisions have already unseated their 2009 estimates. There are a number of other challenges that one could mount.

The authors take into account the improvement in competitiveness in 2008, but not the similar improvement in competitiveness that occurred in 2009. Their assumption about world trade growth could also be regarded as parsimonious. They assume a trend rate of 5% a year whereas a case could be made on the basis of past trends for 6% or more.

Against these points, there is another that works in the opposite direction. The authors' projections imply that none of the loss of output suffered by the economy in 2008 and 2009 is made up over the projection period. This might be a perfectly reasonable assumption. But I believe a policy maker would want to know what shape the balance of payments would be in at current levels of competitiveness were UK activity to return to a level consistent with past trends – which are typically assumed to comprise something like 2% productivity growth and 2½% GDP growth.

Ideally one would try to quantify these points by re-running the model, but an approximate answer is possible using the rules of thumb helpfully provided in the paper. Allowing for a higher rate of world trade growth (taken from 2007) and 2009 levels of competitiveness, I can strip about 2 percentage points off the projected 2020 deficit. UK output is also higher as a result, but not by sufficient a margin to restore GDP to a level consistent with 2½% annual growth after 2007. In addition to the 2009 level of competitiveness and higher world trade, I therefore need to contemplate a higher level of domestic spending sufficient to remove the UK's output gap. Overall I calculate that the 2020 trade balance would be about ½ percentage point of GDP *worse* than the authors' baseline. These adjustments should give some reassurance that the authors have not been unduly pessimistic about the trade account.

This leaves the thorny question of investment income, the rise of which the authors failed to anticipate in their earlier projections. In view of the very considerable difficulties of measuring and projecting investment income, an alternative strategy is to subject the authors' assumptions to a stress test. From this the conclusion I draw is that the magnitude of any further increase in investment income would have to be very large to undermine the authors' basic message.

One could imagine investment income rising as a share of GDP at the unusually fast pace of advance seen over the decade to 2007. In this case, investment income share would rise to 3½% of GDP by 2020. This would be higher than any year in the post-war era although lower than in the exceptional pre-war years when the UK was still a dominant economy on the world stage with huge overseas assets. The effect of the higher investment income would be to reduce the projected 2020 deficit ratio by over 2 percentage points. After allowing for the other changes I have mentioned – to world trade, competitiveness and the UK's output gap – one would be left with a current account deficit close to 3% of GDP. Arguably, this is not sufficient an improvement to remove concerns about the UK's external position.

Moreover, such figures disguise the UK's financing needs. Overseas investment income includes the profits earned but then retained by the branches and subsidiaries of UK multinationals (and excludes comparable retentions of foreign multinationals operating in the UK). These net retentions properly count towards the UK's gross domestic income and the build up of the UK's overseas assets, but by definition they do not reduce *directly* the capital required to finance the external deficit. In the balance of payments statistics, foreign direct investment (FDI) profit retentions count as capital outflows. If investment income is very high, FDI retentions are also likely to be very high. A current account deficit of 3% of GDP cushioned by very high levels of investment income might come with an external financing requirement of 7% of GDP. I think this would put the UK into the danger zone.

I agree with the authors that all such projections must be taken with a large pinch of salt. However, we know that the UK has to undergo a large structural adjustment as the oil runs out; we are rightly concerned that the banking sector may not fill the gap; we know that the UK appears to suffer from a disparity in trade elasticities – with the import elasticity higher that the export elasticity – and we also know that there are asymmetric adjustment pressures. Capital market pressures placed on deficit countries to adjust can be much greater than the pressure applied to surplus countries. This means the costs of being over-concerned about the UK's balance of payments position may well be less than the costs of being under-concerned.

In my view, risk-averse policy makers should have regard to measures that are more likely to benefit Britain's balance of payments than to make it worse. This I take to be the main message of Ken and Bob's excellent strategic analysis.

References

Adams, F.G. (2009), "Will Economic Recovery Drive up World Oil Prices? Growth versus resource availability and the world petroleum market", *World Economics*, Vol. 10, No. 2, pp. 1-26.

Bergsten, C.F. (2002), "Can the United States afford the tax cuts of 2001?", paper presented to a roundtable at the annual meeting of the American Economic Association, 5 January, Atlanta, Georgia.

Birol, F. (2009), Interview with Dr Fatish Birol, chief economist at the International Energy Association , *Independent*, 3 August.

Clarida, R., Goretti, M. and Taylor, M.P. (2007), "Are There Thresholds of Current Account Adjustment in the G7?" in Clarida R. (ed.), *G7 Current Account Imbalances Sustainability and Adjustment*, Chicago: University of Chicago Press, pp. 169-204.

Cosh, A., Hughes, A. and Rowthorn, R.E. (1993), "The competitive role of UK manufacturing industry: 1979-2003" in Hughes, K. (ed.), *The Future of UK Competitiveness and the Role of Industrial Policy*, London: Policy Studies Institute pp. 7-27.

Cosh, A.D., Hughes, A. and Rowthorn, R.E. (1994), "The competitive role of UK manufacturing industry 1950-2003: a case analysis", University of Cambridge, mimeo.

Cosh, A., Coutts, K. and Hughes, A. (1996), "Manufacturing, the balance of payments, and capacity" in Michie, J. and Grieve Smith, J. (eds), *Creating Industrial Capacity: towards full employment*, Oxford: Oxford University Press, pp. 53-71.

Coutts, K., Glyn, A. and Rowthorn, R. (2007), "Structural change under New Labour", *Cambridge Journal of Economics*, Vol. 31, No. 6, November.

DTI (2007), *Meeting the Energy Challenge: A White Paper on Energy*, Department of Trade and Industry, May.

Freund, C. and Warnock, F. (2007), "Current Account Deficits in Industrial Countries: The Bigger They Are, The Harder They Fall?" in Clarida, R. (ed.), *G7 Current Account Imbalances Sustainability and Adjustment*, Chicago: University of Chicago Press, pp. 169-204.

HM Treasury (2009a), *Budget 2009: the economy and public finances – supplementary material*, April.

HM Treasury (2009b), *Budget 2009: Financial Statement and Budget Report*, Chapter B. April.

IMF (2009), *World Economic Outlook, October 2009: sustaining the recovery,* Washington, International Monetary Fund.

Kesler, S. (2007), *Mineral Supply and Demand into the 21st Century,* http://pubs.usgs.gov/circ/2007/1294/reports/paper9.pdf

ONS (2009a), *United Kingdom Balance of Payments (The Pink Book) 2009 Edition*, Office for National Statistics, London: Palgrave MacMillan.

ONS (2009b), *Statistical Bulletin, Balance of Payments 2nd quarter 2009*, Office for National Statistics.

Rowthorn, R.E. and Wells, J.R. (1987), *De-industrialisation and Foreign Trade*, Cambridge: Cambridge University Press.

Rowthorn, R.E. (2009), "Manufacturing and the Balance of Payments" in Lea, R. (ed.) *Nations Choose Prosperity: why Britain needs an industrial policy*, London: Civitas.

Weale, M. (2009), "Growth Prospects and Financial Services", *National Institute Economic Review*, No. 207, January, pp. 4-8.

Notes

Prospects for the UK Balance of Payments

[1] See Rowthorn and Wells (1987).

[2] The members of the group were Alan Hughes, Ken Coutts, Andy Cosh and Robert Rowthorn. Publications of the group include: Cosh, Hughes and Rowthorn (1993, 1994) and Cosh, Coutts and Hughes (1996).

[3] The econometric work for this projection was done by Ken Coutts.

[4] For most of the period since 1971 the balance of trade in manufactures has steadily deteriorated. The two major exceptions, 1990-95 and 2007-2008 were both episodes where major recessions occurred combined with real devaluation of the exchange rate.

[5] UK net investment income is income credits *minus* income debits. If foreign banks operating in London lose money, this counts as a negative debit and has the effect of increasing UK *net* income. Net investment income from *direct* investment is also difficult to interpret, because measurement conventions regarding the finance of direct investment affect what gets counted as income from direct investment. See Coutts, Glyn and Rowthorn (2007).

[6] For further information on our projections see Rowthorn (2009).

[7] Ken Coutts has once again done the modelling and econometric work,

[8] The projections rely on an assessment, based on past relationships, of the main macroeconomic factors (such as income and relative prices) that influence the long-term trends in the balance of payments. See the Appendix.

[9] The impact of the crisis on the financial sector as a whole is discussed in Weale (2009).

[10] HM Treasury (2009b) paragraph B92. Official statistics for the first half of 2009 are consistent with this assumption (ONS 2009b, table B).

[11] The UK has a surplus on high paying direct investment and a deficit on other types of investment. The country gains by borrowing cheap and lending dear. For

information on rates of return on different kinds of asset and liability see ONS (2009a), figures 1.8 and 1.9.

[12] DTI (2007), p. 109, Figure 4.2

[13] Following a detailed assessment of global reserves, the International Energy Association now believes that world oil production could peak as early as 2020 (Birol, 2009). Future oil and mineral prices are discussed in Adams (2009) and Kesler (2007) respectively. Appendix 1.1 of IMF (2009) considers medium-term commodity market prospects.

Commentary

[1] 'In My View', *Observer*, 23 August 2009.

[2] Clarida, Goretti and Taylor, (2007), "Are There Thresholds of Current Account Adjustment in the G7" in *G7 Current Account Imbalances*, pp. 169-200.

[3] The elasticity of manufactured exports with respect to world trade is close to 1, but falls to 0.6 after allowing for the extra imports that extra exports induce. The elasticity for manufactured imports with respect to domestic spending varies over time but averages about 1.4.

[4] Houthakker, H. and Magee, S. (1969), "Income and Price Elasticites in World Trade", *The Review of Economics and Statistics*, Vol. 51, No. 2, May, 111-124.